Original title:
Socks in the Rain

Copyright © 2025 Creative Arts Management OÜ
All rights reserved.

Author: Alexander Thornton
ISBN HARDBACK: 978-1-80586-094-5
ISBN PAPERBACK: 978-1-80586-566-7

## **Traces of Rubber and Rainfall**

Gleeful splashes on the ground,
Puddles giggle all around.
Rubber boots jump, dance with glee,
Oh what fun, just wait and see!

Umbrella upside down, oh dear,
Chasing dreams without a fear.
Slip and slide on streets so wet,
Laughter echoes, no regret.

**Muffled Sounds of a Cloudy Day**


Raindrops tickle on the roof,
Hidden jokes just seek aloof.
Umbrellas whisper 'not today',
As puddles shout 'come out and play!'

Wiggly worms on an outing spree,
Dance a jig so merrily.
Under clouds that seem to pout,
Rainy fun is what it's about.

## Darkened Pathways of Soft Soles

Wobbly walks on mushy ground,
Laughter bounces all around.
Squishy shoes in every hue,
Who knew runoff could be so blue?

Sidewalks laugh in watery cheer,
Squish and squelch, oh, what a year!
Footprints lead a comical tale,
On a quest where rubber prevails.

**The Comfort of Embracing a Storm**

When the clouds begin to play,
Naughty drops fall every way.
Silly dances in the spray,
Make the grayness feel less sway.

Joyful splatters, a friendly toss,
Embracing storms, we're at no loss.
With every slip and tiny fall,
We cherish laughter most of all.

## The Symphony of Squishy Steps

With each splish, there's a jig,
A dance of wet, unyielding gig.
The feet just squelch, a joyful mess,
Creating laughter, I must confess.

Ducks might quack, they steal the show,
But human rhythms steal the flow.
A puddle splash, an unplanned feat,
Turns every step to a goofy beat.

## Treading Through Glistening Streets

The pavement glimmers, oh what fun,
With every step, the laughter's spun.
Jumping high, we aim for fowl,
As rain descends, we guffaw and howl.

A puddle's challenge, bold and bright,
To leap across in sheer delight.
But who would guess, the splash erupts,
And with that surge, excited pups.

## Echoes of Fabric in the Urban Rain

In city streets, the echo sings,
Of squishy sound and wobbly flings.
Each step's a note, each splash a cheer,
The wettest rhythm we hold dear.

Umbrellas twirl like dancers grand,
While puddles clap to a soggy band.
A slip, a slide, then giggles loud,
Making music, oh so proud.

## Humidity and Heartfelt Threads

With wisps of mist in drizzled air,
My wet attire, what a lovely scare.
Stitch by stitch, the fabric sings,
In soggy threads, oh joy it brings.

The breeze blows in, a playful tease,
As laughter flutters, floats with ease.
Forget the vibe of fashion's sway,
Let's revel in the rainy play.

## Unfurling Colors in the Gloom

Puddle jumping, oh what a thrill,
Where footwear dances, against your will.
Bright hues splash on the dreary street,
As laughter bubbles with every wet feat.

A squishy squelch, a slippery slide,
In clashing patterns, nowhere to hide.
Each leap a burst of giggles and glee,
As drizzles turn into a comedy spree.

## The Biographies of Wet Walks

Documented by splashes, each step a scene,
In vivid chapters, aqua turns green.
My shoes tell stories of mishaps galore,
Like a rogue wave crashing on the front door.

Footprint novels left on the path,
With tales of mischief and watery math.
Every drop a plot twist, every glide a joke,
In the eccentric library of puddles we stoke.

## The Arts of Muddy Journeys

Creativity blooms in squishy delight,
As muddy canvases cover with spite.
Artistic endeavors of whom do we blame?
Splattered with colors, no two walks the same.

A slip, a spin, oh what a grand show,
In this gallery, laughter steals the low blow.
With each animated fall in the muck,
Embracing the joy, we're down on our luck.

## Garments of a Cloudy Heart

Raindrops tap dance on windows with flair,
Chasing away the cloudy despair.
In fashionable puddles, we take our stance,
Each drip and drop, a slip-up romance.

Wearing patches of fun in vibrant shades,
Our playful parade, in joy it cascades.
With a wink and a grin, we frolic anew,
In garments of laughter from skies ever blue.

## The Symphony of Squishy Soles

Puddles dance beneath my feet,
A soppy tune, oh what a treat!
Each step a splash, a joyful sound,
In rubber shoes, my bliss is found.

Water's rhythm, oh so grand,
Flop and skip upon this land.
Giggling as the splashes fly,
Creating art where rivers lie.

## When Clouds Weep Cotton

Drips and drops fall from high,
They trickle down with a gentle sigh.
My feet get drenched, a soggy fate,
But laughter swells, it's never late.

A springs' bloom o'er puddles wide,
Waltzing joyfully, I take my stride.
Cotton clouds above, so sly,
Make silly squelches my alibi.

## A Tapestry of Muddy Trails

Across the field in squishy shoes,
I leave behind my joyful hues.
Muddy paths, a nature's art,
Each footprint shows my merry heart.

Colors blend; a canvas thrives,
As laughter echoes, my spirit dives.
Jumping wildly, I embrace the muck,
In splattered joy, I'm truly struck.

## Hideaway Beneath Watered Skies

Beneath the gray, I seek the mirth,
In puddles' charm, I find my worth.
A hiding spot where raindrops play,
Adventures bloom on this wet day.

With every trickle, a giggle grows,
Splashing through the fields it flows.
Oh, joyous scenes where laughter thrives,
Amidst the drizzles, I come alive.

## Cooling Embers of Cozy Foot

A squishy step, a splashy dance,
The puddles laugh, they take their chance.
My toes are cold, but spirits bright,
In soggy realms, we find delight.

A squelch, a squish, a comic sound,
As mischief lurks, the hills surround.
With soggy boots and frisky glee,
We wade through streams, feeling so free!

## Murmurs in the Downpour

The raindrops giggle, plop, and play,
My feet join in, they crave the spray.
With every drip, my laughter grows,
A wobbly dance in puddled throes.

From grey skies fall, a shimm'ring sheen,
My wellies leap in this wild scene.
Each tiny storm, a jolly jest,
As nature's jesters pass the test.

## Stormy Soles and Damp Days

Wobbly soles on slippery trails,
I trip and tumble, tell my tales.
Rain's a jester, full of cheer,
With every splash, I lose my fear.

The clouds throw shade, the mud invites,
As laughter echoes, our spirits take flight.
A wiggly prance, a sudden glide,
In slippers soaked, we'll take the ride.

## Textures Under Tumultuous Skies

Textures mingle beneath the gloom,
Wet patterns swirl in nature's room.
A tickle here, a splashy throw,
While mischief dances in the flow.

Drizzles drizzle, puddles gleam,
In dampened bliss, we stitch our dream.
With soggy messes and grinning glee,
We leap in joy, wild and free!

## **Flashes of Color Under Grey Hues**

Puddles laugh and splatter bright,
Where feet dance in sheer delight.
A slip, a slide, a comical race,
With painted toes, we embrace the chase.

Clouds frown, but spirits soar,
With every splash, we seek to explore.
Raindrops play a merry tune,
As boots jump high, like a loony cartoon.

## A Tangle in the Thunder

Lightning crackles, thunder roars,
Yet here we are, ignoring the floors.
Twisted laces, a sprint gone wild,
With giggles echoing, we're barely mild.

Umbrellas flip and flail about,
As laughter drowns each angry shout.
Cacophony of splashes, a zany spree,
Run for cover? No, that's not for me!

## Comfort Amidst the Deluge

While storms rage, we find our place,
In quirky attire, we set the pace.
Brightly patterned and bold with flair,
We leap through puddles without a care.

The soggy cloth hugs like a friend,
As chuckles rise, they never end.
We gather joy in every drop,
In wet adventures, we'll never stop.

## The Rhapsody of Water Spots

Dancing feet leave trails of glee,
On the slick ground, they're wild and free.
Water spots twirl in a gleeful jig,
As laughter blooms from a cheeky dig.

The rain whirls round, we clap and sing,
Caught in joy, like a slingshot fling.
Every misstep, a story to share,
In this wet world, we show we care.

## **Unraveled Patterns in the Mist**

Bright colors clash, oh what a sight,
Dancing through puddles, we take our flight.
Each step a splatter, a marvelous mess,
We giggle at patterns, no need to impress.

Stripes and polka dots, what a grand show,
Each squishy squelch brings more joy than woe.
Round and round we spin, in a comical twirl,
Nature's own dance floor, watch the fun unfurl.

## Pillow-Soft Trails Through the Drizzle

Raindrops tap dance on a floppy top,
Squishy ground beneath, we bounce, we hop.
Clouds roll in like a fluffy parade,
Every splash we make, a hit escapade.

The world grows fuzzy, a dream in grey,
With each little puddle, we start to play.
Laughs bubble up like the drizzle above,
As we squish, splish, like a wet glove.

## Embracing the Gloomy Puddle

A murky mirror reflects our delight,
We leap and we land, oh what a fright!
Grinning at chaos, each drop our friend,
In this soggy world, the joy won't end.

The gloom's just a giggle wrapped in a frown,
Every gleeful hop in our squishy crown.
We embrace the splashes, the wettest of fun,
In our puddly kingdom, we've already won.

## Tattered Memories in the Storm

Worn-out shoes tell tales, that's quite strange,
Through crooks and crannies, our paths rearrange.
With every soggy step, a giggle escapes,
Creating our history with silly shapes.

In a shuffling shuffle, we lose all decorum,
The rain's a wild child with no need for a quorum.
We gather the laughter, like flowers in bloom,
With a chuckle or two, we defy all the gloom.

## **Glistening Paths and Striped Layers**


Puddles splash with glee, so bold,
While stripes of colors start to unfold.
Muddy splatters take their aim,
As laughter dances through the rain.

A leap and land, oh what a sight,
Chasing droplets, pure delight.
Footprints merge, a mixed affair,
The path ahead, a vibrant scare.

Colors clash with a playful zest,
Wobbly squelches, nature's jest.
Sunshine hides, but who would care?
Worn-out shoes thrive in this lair.

With every step, the laughter grows,
As swirling weather proudly shows.
A cheerful mess, we celebrate,
The magic found when skies are great.

## The Hidden Joy of Waterlogged Walks

Raindrops tap a silly song,
On every step, can't go wrong.
A splash confetti, laughter's cheer,
We embrace the puddles near.

The journey's path, a slippery guise,
Each step reveals surprise and sighs.
Giggles echo, footwear squishes,
Together we make rainy wishes.

Waterlogged shoes bring such delight,
In the storm, we find our light.
A hidden joy in mud we find,
For smiles reign when we unwind.

With every drop, our spirits soar,
The fun we seek is seldom bore.
So grab a friend, or two, or three,
And join the dance, be wild and free.

## Worn Edges and Weathered Dreams

Once pristine soles now tell a tale,
Of adventures wild, they never pale.
In sopping streets, they proudly tread,
With worn-out smiles, their colors spread.

Each pebble skipped, a joyful win,
With every wobble, laughter spins.
Puddle surfing becomes a goal,
As ripples echo in our soul.

A rainy day may seem a plight,
But watch us dance, oh what a sight!
With edges rough and hearts so bold,
We cherish memories more than gold.

So, here's to dreams, both wet and wild,
As laughter bubbles, we feel like a child.
In weathered breath, we leap and play,
As rain transforms our dullest day.

## A Dance of Textiles and Raindrops

With every drop, a soft ballet,
The fabric spins in bright array.
Raindrops twirl like little sprites,
While colors waltz on cloudy nights.

Material meets the thunder's roar,
As soggy soles greet puddled floor.
A ragtag crew of textile friends,
In stormy joy, our laughter bends.

Each splash a note, each squish a sound,
In rhythmic chaos, we are bound.
Let's make a mess, let's dance anew,
For in this storm, we find our view.

So bring your joy and let it flow,
With raindrop dances that steal the show.
Together we weave this fabric bright,
In the earth's soft glow, we find our light.

## Puddles of Fabric

On a walk with shoes too shy,
Splashes dance, oh my, oh my!
Colors swirl in joyful cheer,
As soaked cloths begin to tear.

Laughter echoes, hearts collide,
Avoiding streams, we try to glide.
But every leap just makes us pause,
In a soggy game, we find our flaws.

Wringing laughter, squeaks arise,
Footprints trace our silly guise.
Each puddle holds a hidden jest,
In this wet race, we're all the best.

So let the skies pour down their show,
With fabric dreams that sway and flow.
We'll hop and jump, let spirits soar,
In the joy of wet, who could ask for more?

## Whispers of Wet Threads

In the corner, puddles sigh,
Threads of laughter flutter by.
Chasing raindrops, we're not shy,
With damp cloths and spirits high.

Splashes sing a merry tune,
As we dance beneath the moon.
Every jump, a splash, a cheer,
In the wet, we know no fear.

Avoiding streams, we try our best,
But fabric socks, they jest and jest.
With every squish, a giggle bloomed,
In cheerful chaos, we're consumed.

Whispers flow from drenched attire,
In this tempest, we conspire.
Let's make a splash—what a delight,
We'll turn this storm into pure light!

## The Dance of Damp Footwear

Oh, the prance of soggy shoes,
A rhythm found in wetty blues.
With every leap, a splat, a squeak,
Funny dance, so unique!

Glistening droplets lead the way,
A wet ballet in shades of gray.
Twisting, turning, left and right,
We sway and laugh, what pure delight!

Hopping over muddy pools,
We're the wacky, rainy fools.
Every squish a wild refrain,
Our steps create this laughter chain.

So let the heavens freely pour,
We'll twirl and skip, then skip some more.
In the joy of wet escapades,
Our dance forever blissfully wades!

## Strands of Comfort in Stormy Weather

When clouds burst with a splattering grin,
We embrace the chaos, let the fun begin.
Threads snicker as they soak and squish,
In this humor-laden, watery wish.

Each step a giggle, a play on the ground,
Fabrics twirl in a merry round.
They drip with joy as we hurry along,
In the symphony of splashes, we sing our song.

With socks that sag like giggly friends,
We leap through puddles, the laughter never ends.
Bright patterns swirl in a watery dance,
As we navigate our soggy romance.

So let the storms play their silly tune,
In threads of comfort, we'll sway, we'll swoon.
For in the laughter, we're never alone,
In this stormy weather, we playful roam!

## Weathered Steps in a Puddle's Embrace

On a stroll, I took a leap,
Into a puddle, oh so deep!
My shoes gave way, a squishy cheer,
Splashing giggles, what do I hear?

Dancing droplets, playful and spry,
As I waddle, I laugh and sigh.
A splashy ballet, what a surprise,
Through glistening waters, joy multiplies.

Every step, I'm wearing flair,
With drippy socks—a soggy pair!
Who knew wet wool could make me grin?
In a watery world, I dive right in!

My footsteps echo, a soggy tap,
In this squishy game, I'm wearing a cap.
Through puddles bright, I make my way,
With joy unleashed, it's my rainy day!

**Bands of Color Amidst the Gloom**

Colors pop against the gray,
In raindrops, they decided to play.
Reds and blues, orange and green,
A carnival vibe, so unforeseen.

I skip and drip, without a care,
Patterns dancing everywhere!
My feet like rainbows, bright and keen,
Creating chaos, oh what a scene!

Laughing umbrellas, swirling around,
In this vibrant mess, joy is found.
But watch your step, slippery slide,
In this painting, I take pride.

Watercolors blend on the street,
As I twirl in soggy heat.
In puddle paths, we navigate,
With splashes loud, we celebrate!

## The Melody of Wet Wool

A symphony plays in the rain,
As the heavens sing their refrain.
My feet in puddles, they do the dance,
In squishy notes, I take a chance.

Woolen layers hug my toes,
With every drip, the laughter grows.
A concert loud—a bubbly tune,
With cheeky splashes, I'm over the moon!

Soggy socks in their soggy fate,
Are twirling 'round, feeling great.
Their melody floats in playful streams,
As puddles shimmer with silly dreams.

So let's jive in this wet delight,
With splashes forming pure sunlight.
For in this soggy, joyous plight,
Every raindrop brings laughter bright!

## Of Water and Worn Leather

My leather shoes, they sizzle and squelch,
In a wearing battle, oh how they melt!
With every step, a drippy song,
On this merry path, I bounce along.

Raindrops sounding like a drum,
While puddles cheer, they're feeling fun.
A soaking serenade of wet delight,
Squishy boots dancing in the light.

Mismatched patterns, a rainy craze,
As I splash through this colorful haze.
With laughter jiving from my feet,
In soggy boots, I feel complete.

Waterlogged antics, what a sight,
Free to frolic, oh what a flight!
In the puddle's grip, I take a chance,
Embracing every rain-soaked dance!

## Melodies of Damp Soles

Puddles splash like little drums,
My feet dance in perfect sums.
Chasing puddles, what a treat,
With squishy steps, I find my beat.

Gooey mud so slick and sly,
My footwear may just say goodbye.
But laughter bubbles up like rain,
As I slip back into the game.

## Everchanging Tides of Footwear

Flip-flops jump like happy frogs,
While galoshes slip like lazy dogs.
Each step's a giggle wrapped in wet,
A wardrobe dance, a fun vignette.

High tops whirl like breezy kites,
Through puddles deep on cheer-filled nights.
Fashion's thrill with each soaked sigh,
Who knew shoes could learn to fly?

## **Echoes of Joy in the Storm**

Raindrops tap like tiny bells,
Each splash cast strange, sweet spells.
Wet soles sing a sloshing tune,
A serenade to the rainy moon.

Laughter leaps from every stride,
In my heart, I can't abide.
These drippy moments, oh so fine,
A joyful splash, a life divine.

## Wind and Water in Fashion's Dance

A gust begins a silly twirl,
While raindrops play and splash and swirl.
My footwear gleams in nature's jest,
Each soggy sole a quirky guest.

Colors clash like jokes and puns,
As wet adventures spark the fun.
In this storm, with shoes gone wild,
I'm just a giggling, soggy child.

## Hidden Journeys Through Misty Waters

In puddles deep, a daring leap,
Feet flail like fish that cannot sleep.
Wet socks squeak with each quick step,
A dance of drips, a slippery rep.

Umbrellas spin, a comedic sight,
As raindrops plunge, they take a flight.
Waddling ducks join in the fun,
While squishy shoes race to outrun.

A hidden path beneath the gloom,
Where whimsy finds its perfect room.
Splashes echo, laughter's call,
In watery worlds, we'll never fall.

With boggy boots, we stride with flair,
Leaving trails, we venture there.
In every step, a giggling sound,
Where mischief reigns on soggy ground.

## Abandoning Dry Paths

With every puddle, joy unfolds,
Leaving dry trails for stories bold.
Our feet embrace the soggy thrill,
In squelched delight, we chase the chill.

Clouds gather round, they hear our play,
Inventing games as skies turn gray.
We splash in beats, a merry tune,
While raindrops dance like cheerful ruin.

Epic leaps from curb to curb,
Each misstep met with silly blurb.
In this wet world, we trot with glee,
Leaving behind the dry decree.

With laughter loud and spirits high,
We'll conquer storms, just you and I.
In soggy realms, we write our fate,
Where splashes bring a joy innate.

## Chronicles of Watery Footsteps

Once upon a rainy scene,
Socks were heroes – oh, so keen!
They squished and squelched, took every chance,
In puddles deep, they led the dance.

With mighty leaps and tiny splashes,
They trumped all fears, ignoring crashes.
Each soggy squish brought out a grin,
As squishy tales began to spin.

From friendly ducks, to swirling leaves,
In this wet world, imagination weaves.
With every step, a story leads,
In watery paths, adventure breeds.

The ending's near, but laughter stays,
In chronicles of rainy days.
So tread with cheer, embrace the wet,
For soggy journeys bring no regret.

## Soggy Soliloquy under Gloomy Skies

Beneath the gray, my feet do speak,
With every drip, they squeak and leak.
My heart, it leaps through puddles wide,
With laughter bursting, I take pride.

A soliloquy of drenched delight,
As squishy comedies take flight.
They waddle here, they wiggle there,
On soggy paths without a care.

The clouds above, they chuckle low,
As muddy boots collide with flow.
In every step, a playful jest,
My soggy whispers, truly blessed.

What's life without a little splash?
In misty storms, I make a crash.
For with the rain, my spirit thrives,
In soggy tales, my laughter drives.

## The Lament of Soaked Footwear

Oh dear, my pair has lost its cheer,
A squelching sound is all I hear.
Each step I take, a splash and frown,
My footwear's plight, it drags me down.

What once was bright, now dulled with gloom,
They've transformed from style to floral bloom.
In puddles deep, they take a dive,
My spirit's low, but they're alive!

The river's edge, I can't resist,
My shoes take off, they twist and twist.
Each waterlogged, soggy sip,
Is just a slip of fashion's grip.

But when the sun returns to play,
I'll laugh about this gloomy day.
For every drip that makes me sigh,
Is just a tale of footwear, why!

## Gentle Drizzles and Worn-out Threads

A pitter-patter on the ground,
Makes fashion's finest lose their sound.
With every drop they're weighed down slow,
I look at them and shake my toe.

The clouds above might wear a frown,
As fashion's kings feel quite the clown.
My shoes, once proud, now sagging low,
In water's grip, they steal the show.

Oh how they squeak with every tread,
As if to say, we'd rather dread.
These tattered threads, so worn and bold,
Are soggy tales waiting to be told.

Yet in this downpour, joy must sprout,
We'll dance and twist, ignore the route.
In puddles deep, we splash and play,
With soaked attire, we'll seize the day!

## Reflections in Puddle Mirrors

Oh look below, a sight so grand,
My squishy shoes, they sink like sand.
Each puddle shows my style a mess,
Reflecting on this soggy dress.

The rain it dances, makes me grin,
While my bright friend wears a watery skin.
Squishy sounds fill the chilly air,
And yet, it's hard to show despair.

Each puddle hides a secret cheer,
As we leap in with no fear.
The splashes rise to reach the sky,
Our giggles blend with nature's sigh.

These moments shared beneath the gray,
When laughter sings in the fray,
So let them drip and sag and wet,
For joy in splash is not regret!

## **Blues Beneath Our Toes**

In every step, a little slosh,
These soggy steps, they make me nosh.
I take a leap, they squish and squeal,
Beneath my feet, a watery meal.

The rhythm of the rain's embrace,
Makes every puddle a fun-paced race.
With blues they're singing, oh so loud,
Our dancing feet make spirits proud.

Yet laundry day looms in the back,
For soggy shoes take quite the whack.
But here we are, not feeling blue,
As merry splashes bid adieu.

So let us twirl in nature's song,
With every drip, we can't go wrong.
For in this dance of drips and swirls,
We find our joys, as laughter twirls!

## Kinship with the Elements

In puddles, I dance, my fate is wet,
Nature's my partner, no need to fret.
Each splash brings a giggle, a silly delight,
As clouds overhead burst with laughter's light.

Mud hugs my ankles, a squishy embrace,
How silly I look in this marshy place.
Bouncing along, I wave at the sky,
Who knew my best friends would drip from on high?

With each raindrop's journey, I revel and spin,
A messy parade where the fun can begin.
The sun may scold, with its bright, shining glare,
But I'll stick with the puddles, the joy's in the air.

Amidst all the chaos, we twirl side by side,
With every wet footstep, I laugh and I glide.
So here's to our kinship, so joyous and free,
In this merry deluge, just Nature and me.

## In the Midst of Murk

Oh look, I've a river, right down the lane,
Makes walking a challenge, brings giggles from pain.
Two shoes full of water, I squish with a grin,
My socks are rebellious, let the fun begin!

The sky's wearing grey, a comedy show,
As raindrops audition and put on a flow.
With every new puddle, I leap and I whirl,
This joyous mishap puts my heart in a twirl.

Wading through woes, my laughter, a stream,
Amidst all this sadness, I plot my grand scheme.
A splash to the left, a splash back on right,
Dancing in time with the thunder's delight!

This murky chaos, a friend in disguise,
Together we giggle, no angry skies.
For each drip that falls is a chance to break free,
In the midst of the murk, come play next to me!

## **Vibrant Patterns Drenched in Rain**

Oh, look at my outfit, a kaleidoscope sight,
Bright polka dots dancing in drizzles of light.
With every downpour, the colors just pop,
Like a painter with glee, I refuse to stop.

My boots go splashing, a joyous parade,
As puddles turn mirrors for tricks that I've played.
And while it may seem like I'm lost in a spree,
My heart just flutters, wild and carefree.

The puddles are canvases, I'm quite the artist,
With splatters and giggles, I truly am the smartest.
Forget about elegance, poise swept away,
These vibrant adornments are here for the play!

When raindrops conspire, let laughter arise,
Let's twirl in the water, dance under gray skies.
For in these drenched moments, fun does remain,
Life's vibrant patterns shine bright in the rain.

## **The Lullaby of Rain-soaked Steps**

Each raindrop a note in this charming refrain,
As I step out the door to embrace all the rain.
My heart finds a rhythm, a playful parade,
In the symphony sung by the clouds in cascade.

With squishes and splashes, I waltz through the storm,
Each puddle a hug, each drizzle a warm.
The world is my stage and I'm putting on flair,
With laughter and giggles skipping without care.

The thunder, my drummer, beats time with a boom,
As I leap through the showers, creating a room.
A soft, silly lullaby fills the cool air,
In the melody spun by the rain, I declare!

So join in the dance, let your worries dissolve,
In this playful duet, together we'll evolve.
For every wet step, a joyous story we weave,
In the lullaby of rain, let's laugh and believe.

## **Tapestry of a Rainy Wander**

Upon the streets, my feet do splash,
A symphony of squelches, oh what a clash!
With puddles jumping as I glide,
Each step a giggle, my heart filled with pride.

Colors twirl in the gloomy air,
My footwear's a party, quite beyond compare!
Water drips down with a splashy surprise,
While I leap and twirl, with joy in my eyes.

They say it's silly, I should feel ashamed,
But splashing about, oh, I'm uncontained!
The world is a canvas, my feet are the brush,
In this puddle dance, I'll never rush.

So let the clouds grumble, let the skies cry,
With every footfall, my spirits fly high!
In the tapestry woven with laughter and cheer,
I'll dance in my colors, with nothing to fear.

## Musings of a Cozy Covering

In the cozy nook where warmth combines,
A tale of coverings and whimsical designs.
Huddled together, the fabric brigade,
As droplets patter, we chuckle and jade.

Patterns of polka and stripes in a row,
Face the rain's challenge with nary a woe.
With mismatched charm and hearts full of glee,
We twirl through the puddles, as merry can be.

Plucky companions in colors so bright,
We waddle and wiggle, what a glorious sight!
Each step is an echo of laughter and fun,
Embracing the splashes till the day is done.

Oh, trials of water won't dampen our cheer,
For we are the warriors of frivolous dear!
So raise up your arms, let the merriment sound,
In our cozy fortress, joy knows no bound!

## Whispers of Wet Fabrics

Beneath the clouds, with shadows that creep,
Wet threads chatter as puddles leap.
Whispers of fabric, they dance with delight,
As I skip through the puddles, a jovial sight!

Colors collide in a wet ballet,
What splashes they conjure on this drizzly day!
Flamboyant textures, oh what a spree,
With every drip-drop, they're laughing with me.

A splash, a tinkle, a twirl in the mist,
Who knew that soaking could feel like bliss?
We'll shimmy and shake while the world looks on,
Creating a ruckus until the dawn.

So here's to the laughter that droplets bring,
In this wet wonderland, I'll dance and I'll sing!
With whispers of fabrics, I'll prance and sway,
For in this soggy joy, I'll gladly stay.

## Dancing Through Puddles

With every splash, a new note resounds,
I'm the conductor of splishy-splash sounds.
Raindrops are rhythm, my feet lead the way,
Dancing through puddles, come what may!

Donning a grin and my fanciest trims,
I stomp through the water, abandon all whims.
Around all the whirlpools, I twirl and I wheel,
In this merry dance, oh, what a feel!

The world feels lighter, as laughter takes flight,
With the sky giggling, the weather's just right.
Each swish, each slosh, paints a story anew,
In this playful parade, I gallop right through.

So join me, dear friends, on this whimsical ride,
Where puddles are portals, they'll never divide!
We'll wade through the laughter, the giggles will swell,
In the dance of the droplets, we'll bubble like gel!

## Where Fabric Meets the Flood

A puddle's gleeful splash calls me,
As squishy fabric gives a plea.
Dancing feet in soggy shoes,
Such joyous chaos, who could snooze?

Waterlogged cotton twirls with glee,
Oh, what a sight for all to see!
The dance party starts, no time to fret,
In soggy attire, no regret yet.

My toes wiggle in the chilly spray,
With every step, I'm led astray.
Laughter erupts as I trip and slide,
Fabric chaos, a slippery ride!

So let it pour, let the heavens burst,
In this soggy world, I'm immersed.
With each splash, joy finds its way,
In the flood, we'll dance and play!

## Hues of the Overcast Walk

Gray clouds loom, but spirits soar,
Each step makes puddles roar!
Umbrella hats and mismatched shoes,
We'll strut through rain without a bruise!

Squishy tread on the asphalt bright,
In this damp world, we'll take flight.
Rainbow socks with polka dots,
Bring on the giggles, forget the knots!

Drizzled skies can't dampen our jest,
Witty remarks put humor to the test.
Wobbling steps like we're on a cruise,
We paint the world in vibrant hues!

With puddles jumping, we march ahead,
In wet fabric, we lay our bed.
Laughter bubbles in every splash,
In these damp moments, we make a splash!

## Laughter Beneath Umbrellas

Beneath our canopies, we giggle and sway,
Against the drizzle, we frolic and play.
Splashes arise, creating a show,
With each droplet, our spirits grow.

Umbrellas bob like ships at sea,
Dodging raindrops gleefully.
Dripping ends and soggy socks,
Who knew we could dance in frosty blocks?

Friends linked together in ridiculous style,
Puddles jump, they beguile!
Laughter rises as we squat and leap,
In this watery jest, we'll make a heap!

Under the storm, we find a song,
Each splash a note, we'll sing along.
So hold your umbrellas and let's rejoice,
In the rain's rhythm, we've found our voice!

## **Fleeting Steps on a Wet Canvas**

Each step I take leaves a mark behind,
On this squishy canvas, I'm intertwined.
Laughing at puddles, my playful foe,
In every splash, I let my joy flow.

Dancing like drips from the eaves above,
With rubber boots, I find my groove.
Slick streets echo with our delight,
As laughter refills the morning light.

Trail of colors as I twirl and dash,
Every drop my own little splash.
Wet shoes squawk like a chorus of cheer,
In this wacky world, I have no fear!

So here's to the rain, a canvas so bold,
Painting memories worth more than gold.
With laughter as my guide, I take each leap,
Across this wet canvas, my joys I'll keep!

## Journeying in Tattered Threads

Wandering in quirky footwear,
One's left sock is pink, quite a flare.
The other one's blue, what a clash!
Splashing through puddles, making a splash!

The squishy sound with every step,
Laughing at how they miskept.
Each foot slips, then regains sway,
Adventures unfold in a silly way!

Dashing under a dawn's wet sky,
Who knew fashion could bring such a high?
Wobbly grooves on this rainy dance,
Here's to mismatched love, not a chance!

With every drip, grins grow wide,
Worn-out threads our unifiers applied.
Tripping on dreams in every puddle,
Life's a giggle, let's not go muddle!

## Trudging Toward Tomorrow

Every trail leads to splatter and muck,
Stomping through puddles, wishing for luck.
Clunky clogs shout with each cheer,
Life's a comic, let laughter steer!

Taking on puddles, some twenty feet wide,
With every misstep, our giants abide.
Beneath cloudy skies, we trip and we slip,
Bound together in this joyful quip!

Cheerful chaos, we chase the delight,
In our mismatched shoes, oddly uptight.
But here come the clouds with a thundering roar,
Who knew blunders could open such doors!

So we trudge on with our heads held high,
Laughing at the weather, we will not cry.
Braving tomorrow, we'll dance in the rain,
With hearts full of giggles, we'll never be plain!

# Embracing the Unruly Weather

Pitter-patter leads the way,
Dancing feet in a splashy play.
In colorful garb, we leap about,
Daring dampness, there's no doubt!

With the sun playing hide and seek,
We barter grins against the bleak.
Over puddles we soar, a gallant glide,
The world's our puddle, with joy as our guide!

Sloshing through streets, the laughter ignites,
Our misfit shoes make grand highlights.
Soak to the skin, yet spirits are bright,
In this unruly weather, we embrace our light!

Each splatter a badge of our merry quest,
With every little blunder, we're truly blessed.
Waltzing with raindrops, we make our mark,
In the carnival of puddles, we'll dance until dark!

## The Footprints of Forgotten Storms

In little nooks where puddles lie,
Echoes of laughter float through the sky.
With squelching steps, we rise and fall,
Our slippery path becomes a ball!

Every splosh creates a tune so sweet,
As threads dampen, we fly on our feet.
Gone are the worries, lost in the slide,
Who knew that wet feet could fill us with pride?

Memory prints left on this lane,
We can't help but giggle at our silly gain.
While stories of storms drift on the breeze,
We laugh at the chaos, doing as we please!

Tracing through puddles, feet in a whirl,
Let's write the history of how we twirl.
When laughter is found 'neath the stormy veil,
The footprints of joy are never stale!

## Colors Running in the Monsoon

A puddle splashes, bright and bold,
The hues of mismatched tales unfold.
Polka dots dance in muddy streams,
As laughter plays in playful beams.

Each step a squeeze, a giggle flows,
With every leap, the water shows.
Flashing reds, and yellows too,
Splashing joy—who needs a shoe?

The rainbow's lost and found is here,
On squishy grass, we persevere.
With colors running, hearts align,
In this wild wash, we feel divine.

So let it pour, the jokes will fly,
With vivid whims beneath the sky.
In this squelching, joyful spree,
Nothing seems to bother me.

## Little Journeys Through the Deluge

Umbrellas bob and hats askew,
A marathon of muddy view.
Tiny rafts on curbs we see,
Floating boats of fantasy.

Each rush of water, a thrilling ride,
Giggles echo—it's our guide.
Stomping feet, a froggy dance,
In every splash, a silly chance.

We leap from curb to soggy lane,
Steering clear of watery bane.
Little journeys, wide and grand,
In this chaos, we take a stand.

Every drop is a silly cheer,
With splashes loud, we have no fear.
In this watery wild, we play,
Each moment brightens up the gray.

**Creases of Comfort on Shiny Pavements**

Shiny streets reflect the gray,
Where puddles chat and kids all play.
The sidewalks glisten, tales retold,
Of cozy days, in laughter bold.

Creased companions dance with glee,
Their colors flashing, wild and free.
Each soppy slip, a merry sight,
Brings forth giggles—pure delight.

A splash attack, a friendly race,
With puddles deep, we find our place.
Soaked yet smiling, what a scene,
In every squish, pure joy we glean.

Windswept hair and muddy toes,
In storms like these, adventure grows.
The shiny paths, a canvas wide,
For silly tales, we take in stride.

## The Cloak of Clouds & Comfort

Underneath the cloudy cloak,
Laughter rises with each stroke.
Dressed in splashes, brave and bold,
Each step a story to be told.

Waterfalls drip from noses bright,
As puddles gleam and spirits light.
Clutch our friends, we twirl and spin,
In this drizzy dance, we win.

Kicking up the dampened earth,
Find our joy, our simple worth.
Bubbles form with every hop,
In playful jests, we can't be stopped.

The clouds may grumble, winds might howl,
Yet we'll greet them with a bow.
In this downpour, laughter reigns,
With every drop, a smile remains.

## Underfoot: A Tale of Water's Touch

With splashes and puddles, my feet take a leap,
They dance through the droplets, in laughter we seep.
A whoosh and a whirl, I twirl to the side,
My shoes, oh they giggle, can't hold them with pride.

Two friends on a journey, they drag through the muck,
Each step is a maze, oh what wobbly luck!
We bounce like rubber, defying the tide,
While the world just stares, and the clouds seem to chide.

A heartfelt connection, where humor finds play,
In puddle-filled moments, we slosh on our way.
And though we get soggy, we laugh 'til we ache,
For every wet step is a new chance to shake.

So here's to the journey, the squishy delight,
In drizzles and fumbles, we share pure delight.
A voyage of folly, so vividly bright,
With each misty giggle, our joy takes to flight.

## Chasing Rainbows Through the Drizzle

In rain's gentle patter, adventure begins,
With every small splash, a new joy that spins.
We jump like the raindrops, carefree and spry,
Creating our own show as puddles comply.

The sun peeks through clouds, a trickster in play,
While laughter erupts, sending worries away.
Oh, the wobbly dance, it brings such a cheer,
As squishy surprises await us right here.

With each little puddle comes laughter anew,
As friends skip together, like ducks in a queue.
So here's to the drizzle, in all of its glee,
For every wet moment, we let ourselves be.

Through storms we'll keep frolicking, gleaming with light,

With joy in our pockets, the world feels just right.
A chase for the colors that shimmer and shine,
In the heart of the rain, we find our design.

## Threads That Meet the Wet Ground

Threads dance and flutter, in a stormy embrace,
With each little splash, there's a most clumsy grace.
They twist and they turn, while puddles explode,
Creating a circus, a clumsy road show.

The water's a trickster, my feet start to squirm,
As I wade through confusion, wobbly and firm.
The floor turns to waves, a slippery thrill,
As I shuffle and slide, against nature's will.

With giggles a-plenty, we relish the game,
No need for dry footing, it's all just the same.
There's silly delight in each tiny slip,
And the cheerful wet sounds, like a sweet comic trip.

So rally your buddies, let's embrace the jest,
In this merry muck dance, we'll find our best fest.
We'll frolic through puddles, and sing out with cheer,
Each drippy adventure, with laughter sincere.

## Mirth in the Downpour

In droplets of laughter, we find our own way,
As raindrops do tickle, we twirl and sway.
A splash here, a slip there, it's all meant for fun,
Each crinkle of fabric, a laugh that's well-spun.

With giggles and splashes, our worries dissolve,
In drizzles of joy, our spirits revolve.
The clouds may be grumpy, but we find our delight,
In mirth of the moment, we dance in the night.

A journey through water, where hilarity flows,
Each step is a story that laughter bestows.
When puddles are beckoning, we answer their call,
In this whimsical downpour, we love it all.

So gather your pals, let's create a parade,
In puddles and splashes, we'll never be swayed.
For in every wet second lies pure joy and cheer,
With mirth in the downpour, we wash away fear.

## Journeying with Flimsy Covers

In a puddle deep, my foot did dive,
A squishy surprise, oh how I thrive!
A splash of water, a laugh so bright,
My mismatched friends give quite a fright.

Dripping wool and cotton blend,
A dance of colors, round the bend.
Each step I take, a squelch, a smile,
For soggy journeys, I'd walk a mile.

Who needs shoes when squish is grand?
A rubber ducky, my trusty band!
We'll waddle through streets, no care to hide,
In this flashy parade, I'm soaked with pride.

So grab your raincoat, let's make a splash,
Through stormy weather, we'll make a bash!
With flimsy covers, we'll take on the brave,
In waterlogged fun, we'll always rave!

## Stories Etched in Wet Fabric

With every dribble, a tale unfolds,
Of socked adventures, where laughter molds.
My feet start to spin, in circles so round,
The world's a stage, where mud is unbound.

A slippery tram, we slide side to side,
While onlookers giggle, their chuckles collide.
The patterns alive, no dullness in sight,
As puddles whisper, 'This is pure delight!'

Woolly memories held tight with glee,
Each drop a chapter, forever carefree.
Who knew fabric could hold such a tale?
In drenching downpours, my spirits won't pale.

With every step, more stories emerge,
In these soaking tales, my heart starts to surge.
As clouds start to giggle and streams start to fray,
I dance in the downpour, come join the ballet!

## Natural Prints of a Rainy Day

There's magic in water, it paints on my feet,
Every puddle's a canvas, where colors compete.
Stripes of green and a splash of gray,
Artistry blooms in the mud where I play.

Wobbly wildlife parade on the street,
In dappled attire, I'm stylin' with heat.
An umbrella twirls, a hat's in the fray,
With nature's own prints on this wacky day!

Elastic surprises, a squish with a scream,
The path comes alive, in a watery dream.
A twist and a turn, look at those feet,
Sprinkling laughter, in rhythmic repeat.

Come dance in the puddles, feel the delight,
With drizzles and giggles, we'll dance through the night.
In this soggy escapade, we'll find our way,
Creating grand patterns, come join the play!

## Footfalls and Drizzles Intertwined

In the midst of raindrops, my steps keep a beat,
With every footfall, I can't help but greet.
The splashes like music, a catchy refrain,
On this journey of jests, we smile through the rain.

With bounces and giggles, my shoes start to squish,
Opening umbrellas, fulfilling a wish.
While others stay dry, we're splashing with flair,
Insisting the rain is the best kind of air.

Dribbles and drapes weave tales on the ground,
As squishy surprises come jostling around.
A puddle jumps up, a shimmery gleam,
In the world of footfalls, it's all just a dream!

So join in this laughter, don't worry, don't flee,
Let the drizzles tattoo, just you and me.
For when the downpours come, we'll never confine,
We'll dance through the droplets, our hearts in a line!

## Silken Spills and Earthy Tones

A puddle plops, a splash so neat,
My feet get cozy, oh what a treat!
In colors bright, they twist and swirl,
Like dancing gals in a silly whirl.

With patterns wild and polka dots,
Each step's a giggle, oh, what have we got?
A mishap here, a squeak with glee,
These plushy companions, so wild and free.

The sun may hide, but spirits soar,
With every plunge, we laugh some more.
Who knew a stroll could lighten the day,
In squishy shoes, we'll jump and play!

Sohere we stand, making delight,
With merry feet, we'll dance through light.
Let droplets fall, let laughter reign,
For joy in splashes shall still remain.

## Quagmire of Comfort

In slimy pools where trouble brews,
I find my cheer in yucky hues.
A flick, a flop, a slip and slide,
My trusty gear, my joyful ride.

Each step a squelch, a comical cheer,
With mud-streaked style, I persevere.
The miry path, a silly jest,
My feet in fits of pure unrest.

With every drift, I start to grin,
For wobbly steps bring laughter in.
Forget the worries, the woes of fate,
These muddy moments, oh how they rate!

So call me goofy, or maybe mad,
But in this chaos, I'm simply glad.
With all this mess, I dance with glee,
In my squishy bliss, I feel so free!

## Cascades of Softness Underfoot

With every rain, a treasure blooms,
A slippery world that laughs and zooms.
My feet, they wiggle, my heart's aglow,
As puddles chuckle and water flows.

They slip and slide in a playful spree,
In cushy warmth, they twirl with glee.
The drizzle drips and blurs the line,
Of one, two, three—let's dance, divine!

In fluffy layers, I waddle and tread,
With playful mischief in every spread.
Softness thunders like joyous rain,
My squishy socks, oh, who needs disdain?

So splash about, let laughter sound,
In bouncy forms and squelching ground.
A ticklish dance, let's break away,
In this soft storm, we'll laugh and play!

## An Elegy for the Overcast

Oh dreary skies, with clouds that loom,
But fear not, my friends, there's joy in gloom!
With every drip that falls like fate,
We laugh aloud and celebrate.

In hues of gray, our spirits lift,
As puddles gather, a wonderful gift.
Each splash a jest, a chuckle loud,
In this wet world, we dance unbowed.

With lollipop stripes and wacky checks,
Our outfits gleam, ignoring wrecks.
Who needs the sun when fun's at hand?
Let raindrops form a merry band!

So shall we waltz with squishy flair,
In soggy shoes, we won't despair.
For life's a joke, we snicker and spin,
In overcast joy, the thrill begins!

## Threads of Gloomy Days

Wet feet tap a silly tune,
Dancing puddles shape the gloom.
Each droplet whispers a jest,
Who knew rain could be a fest?

Puddles deep, a splashing spree,
Turn my shoes to boats at sea.
Each step's a squish, a funny fright,
As I leap left, then jump right.

Umbrellas spin like tops in tow,
Giggles echo, high and low.
Bring on the drizzle, come what may,
These soggy shoes will laugh all day.

So let the clouds unleash their play,
Joy in the puddles, come what may.
Forget the gloom, let's prance and slide,
In this wet world, let's take a ride!

## The Cacophony of Sloshing Steps

Footsteps squelch in rhythmic tone,
A melody of drips alone.
Each stride a symphony so grand,
In wobbly footwear, let's make a stand.

Rainy beats on lonely streets,
With splashes that sound like happy tweets.
Giggles spill with every splash,
In puddles deep, we carefree dash.

The water's chorus sings aloud,
While I parade beneath the cloud.
Each plop and pop, a comedy scene,
In rubber boots, I'm king and queen.

Oh, what a sight in torrents of play,
With laughter leading the wet ballet.
Drowning worries with every glance,
Join my soggy, silly dance!

## Damp Delight on City Streets

Feet that flop and flop away,
Wiggle-waggling in the spray.
Giggles sprout from every lane,
As we boogie in the rain.

Rain hats wobble, umbrellas flip,
Wiggling bodies start to trip.
Puddles beckon, a slippery invite,
Come join the fun, forget the fright!

City lights in drops reflect,
Sopping shoes that we neglect.
With every step, a splash will flare,
What a mess! But who would care?

Damp delight, a joyous call,
Laughing loud, let raindrops fall.
Embrace the wet, wear it proud,
In this soggy dance, we're loud!

# Cozy Comforts in Drizzle

A cozy nook with windows wide,
Sipping cocoa, feeling pride.
Elbows on the sill, let's cheer,
For puddles form with rain so near.

The soft patter on my roof,
Matches rhythms of my goof.
Each squish and slosh, a giggle treat,
As I brave the storming street.

Rain-soaked laughter fills the air,
Every splash, a tiny scare.
But together, we'll march on through,
Finding joy in every blue.

So let the drizzle dance around,
In silly moments, joy is found.
With warm hearts and laughter bright,
We'll cherish wet days, pure delight!

www.ingramcontent.com/pod-product-compliance
Lightning Source LLC
Chambersburg PA
CBHW070317120526
44590CB00017B/2717